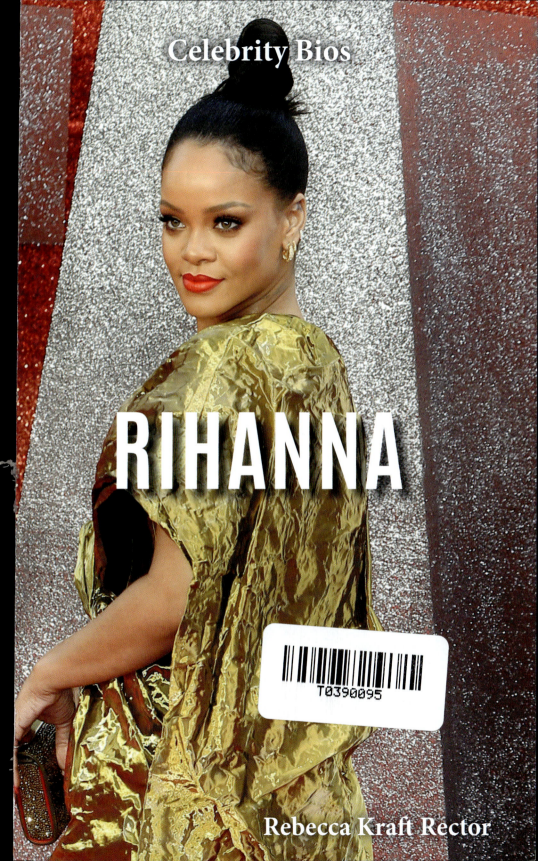

WWW.APEXEDITIONS.COM

Copyright © 2025 by Apex Editions, Mendota Heights, MN 55120. All rights reserved. No part of this book may be reproduced or utilized in any form or by any means without written permission from the publisher.

Apex is distributed by North Star Editions:
sales@northstareditions.com | 888-417-0195

Produced for Apex by Red Line Editorial.

Photographs ©: Fred Duval/SOPA Images/Sipa USA/AP Images, cover, 1; Ryan Kang/AP Images, 4–5; Ross D. Franklin/AP Images, 6–7; Shutterstock Images, 8–9, 10–11, 16–17, 18–19, 28–29, 44–45, 46–47, 50–51, 58; Jacques Langevin/AP Images, 12–13; Christopher Polk/Getty Images Entertainment/Getty Images, 14–15; Chris Pizzello/AP Images, 20–21, 48–49; Chris Carlson/AP Images, 22–23; Walter Bieri/Keystone/AP Images, 24–25; Roberto Pfeil/AP Images, 27; Kevork Djansezian/AP Images, 30–31; Al Messerschmidt/AP Images, 32–33; Matt Sayles/AP Images, 34–35; Charles Sykes/Invision/AP Images, 36–37; Logan Bowles/AP Images, 39; Matt Sayles/Invision/AP Images, 40–41; Evan Agostini/Invision/AP Images, 42–43; DPRF/Star Max/IPx/AP Images, 52–53; Steven Senne/AP Images, 54–55; EMPPL PA Wire/AP Images, 56–57

Library of Congress Control Number: 2023922481

ISBN
979-8-89250-218-4 (hardcover)
979-8-89250-239-9 (paperback)
979-8-89250-279-5 (ebook pdf)
979-8-89250-260-3 (hosted ebook)

Printed in the United States of America
Mankato, MN
082024

NOTE TO PARENTS AND EDUCATORS

Apex books are designed to build literacy skills in striving readers. Exciting, high-interest content attracts and holds readers' attention. The text is carefully leveled to allow students to achieve success quickly.

TABLE OF CONTENTS

Chapter 1
A HUGE PERFORMANCE 5

Chapter 2
A GIRL CALLED ROBYN 9

Chapter 3
RISING TO THE TOP 17

In the Spotlight
FROM DEMO TO SMASH HIT 26

Chapter 4
SUPERSTAR 28

In the Spotlight
"UMBRELLA" 38

Chapter 5
BRANCHING OUT 41

Chapter 6
A STRONG LEGACY 50

FAST FACTS • 59
COMPREHENSION QUESTIONS • 60
GLOSSARY • 62
TO LEARN MORE • 63
ABOUT THE AUTHOR • 63
INDEX • 64

Stylist Jahleel Weaver helped create Rihanna's Super Bowl look.

Chapter 1

A HUGE PERFORMANCE

It's February 2023. Rihanna stands on a platform in the air. She holds a mic. The Super Bowl halftime show is about to begin. It's Rihanna's first performance in seven years. But she is ready.

The music starts. Rihanna's platform rises higher. Above the crowd, Rihanna starts to sing. She performs her greatest hits. They blend together into a medley of several songs. Eighty people dance below. More than 67,000 people watch from the crowd. And 121 million people watch on TV. The show is a huge success.

AN IMPORTANT SHOW

Rihanna had been asked to perform the 2019 halftime show. That time, she said no. But in 2022, she had a child. That changed her thoughts. She wanted her son to see her performance. She also wanted to represent Black women, immigrants, and her home.

Rihanna's performance was one of the most viewed halftime shows of all time.

About 280,000 people live in Barbados. The island nation has many beaches.

Chapter 2
A GIRL CALLED ROBYN

Robyn Rihanna Fenty was born on February 20, 1988. She grew up in Barbados. This island nation is in the Caribbean Sea. Robyn lived in St. Michael. This area is in the southwest part of the island.

Robyn lived in a beautiful place. But not everything was perfect. Her father was a drug addict. That caused problems for her family. When Robyn was 14, her parents got divorced. Robyn had strong headaches during that time. They may have been caused by stress.

MAKING MONEY

When Robyn was a kid, her family did not always have a lot of money. Robyn wanted to make more money. So, she sold candy at school. Her family also had a small store on the street. She sold clothes there.

Robyn grew up near Bridgetown. It is the largest town in Barbados.

Bob Marley was a reggae singer. He was one of Robyn's favorite artists as a child.

In other ways, Robyn was happy. At school, she was a good student. She was friendly, and she was a good leader. Robyn also enjoyed music. She liked to sing. She listened to many different genres. Reggae was one of her favorites. She loved R&B, hip-hop, and pop, too.

ONE OF THE BOYS

Robyn grew up with two brothers. She also had 13 male cousins. When she was young, Robyn was a tomboy. She wanted to do what the boys did. She wanted to climb trees and fight.

13

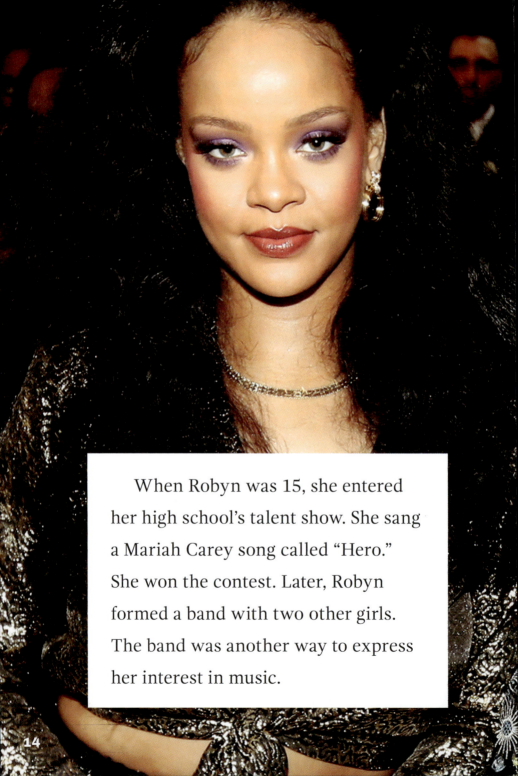

When Robyn was 15, she entered her high school's talent show. She sang a Mariah Carey song called "Hero." She won the contest. Later, Robyn formed a band with two other girls. The band was another way to express her interest in music.

Melissa Forde (right) often attends events with Rihanna.

BEST FRIENDS

Robyn met Melissa Forde when they were 14. The two became best friends. They stayed close for many years. They even got tattoos of each other's birthdays.

Evan Rogers and his producing partner Carl Sturken have worked with many stars, including *NSYNC (pictured).

Chapter 3
RISING TO THE TOP

In 2004, Robyn's band got a big chance. Evan Rogers was in Barbados. He was a music producer from New York. Robyn's band sang for him. Rogers liked the band. But he loved Robyn's singing. He asked her to come to New York and make a demo.

Robyn wanted to go. She dreamed of being a musician. It was all she had ever wanted. Her mother was not so sure. She wanted Robyn to finish school. But when Robyn was 16, she left Barbados. She was ready to take the chance. She reached New York and recorded the demo.

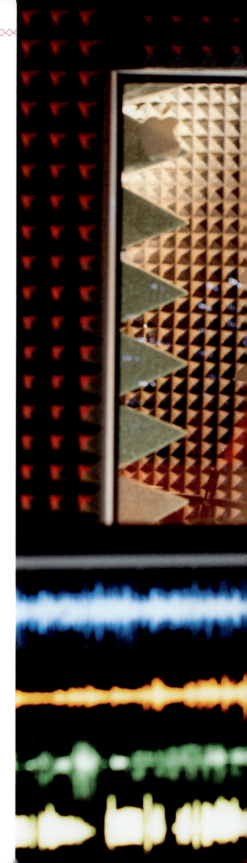

Demos are early drafts of songs. Artists may share them with people and companies that make music.

Rogers sent Robyn's demo to Jay-Z. He was a famous rapper. He was also the head of Def Jam Recordings. Then, Robyn sang for Jay-Z, too. Jay-Z was impressed. He wanted her on his record label. He offered Robyn a contract.

LET'S SIGN NOW

Jay-Z loved Robyn's singing right away. So, he asked for a contract that day. The contract took hours to write. But Robyn stayed until it was ready. She finally left their meeting at 3:00 a.m.

Def Jam Recordings worked with many early hip-hop artists. The company produced records for LL Cool J (pictured) and the Beastie Boys.

Robyn was just 17 years old when "Pon de Replay" was released.

In May 2005, Robyn's first single came out. Her career as Rihanna began. "Pon de Replay" was a worldwide hit. A few months later, her first album came out. It was called *Music of the Sun*. The music was fast and bouncy. It had lots of energy. It was easy to dance to. The album got mixed reviews. But it was a strong start.

A NAME FOR A STAR

Robyn's middle name is Rihanna. It means "great queen" in Irish. Evan Rogers thought the name would be good for a music career. So, Robyn decided to use it. "Rihanna" became her pop-star name.

Rihanna's next album came out in 2006. It was called *A Girl Like Me*. The songs were not just party songs. They showed different emotions. That made it feel more personal to Rihanna. The songs mixed more genres than before, too. The album was a big success. "SOS" was a dance-pop song. It went to the top of the charts.

ON TOUR

In 2005, Rihanna went on her first tour. She sang before the main singer, Gwen Stefani, came onstage. Rihanna toured again in 2006. But this time, she was the headliner. Some shows had thousands of people in the audience.

"SOS" was Rihanna's first No. 1 hit. It stayed at the top of the charts for three weeks in a row.

In the Spotlight

FROM DEMO TO SMASH HIT

"Pon de Replay" uses a Caribbean dialect. The phrase means "play it again." In the song, Rihanna asks the DJ to play the song again and turn the music up.

"Pon de Replay" features sounds from Caribbean genres like dancehall and reggae. The song has strong drumbeats. Rihanna sings repeating lyrics over the beats. At first, Rihanna thought the song sounded like a nursery rhyme. But listeners loved it. They found it fun to listen and dance to.

> "Pon de Replay" rose to No. 2 on the Billboard Hot 100 chart.

Chapter 4

SUPERSTAR

In 2007, Rihanna did not want to appear as young. She wanted to show more grown-up sides of herself. She released her third album. The beats of *Good Girl Gone Bad* were less tropical. The album sounded more like R&B. It showed that Rihanna was bold and strong.

Rihanna won Teen Choice Awards in 2006 and 2007. But she wanted her music to appeal to a wide range of people.

Good Girl Gone Bad included the song "Umbrella." The song was Rihanna's biggest hit yet. Rihanna won a Grammy Award for it. Other songs from the album also reached high on the Billboard charts. The album became a worldwide success. It made Rihanna a superstar.

TEAMING UP

Rihanna worked with several other artists on *Good Girl Gone Bad*. They included Ne-Yo and Justin Timberlake. Jay-Z was another. He rapped on "Umbrella." Later in Rihanna's career, she kept working with other artists. Some of her biggest hits came from these collaborations.

Rihanna was nominated for four Grammy Awards in 2007.

Rihanna helped write nine of the songs on *Rated R*.

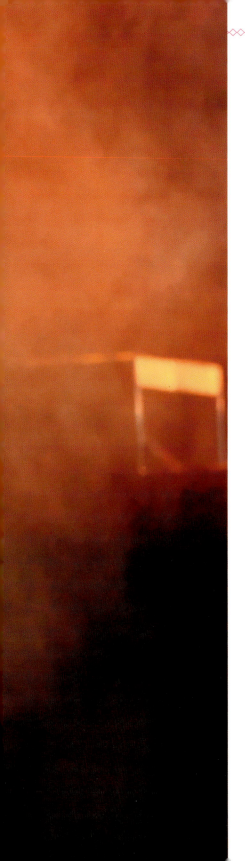

Behind the scenes, Rihanna faced problems. She was in an abusive relationship. In 2009, her boyfriend hit her. They separated, and he was charged with a crime.

This experience was very difficult. Rihanna channeled it into her next album, *Rated R*. This album featured darker songs than her earlier work. Many were top hits. For example, "Rude Boy" became her fifth No. 1 song on the Billboard Hot 100 chart.

After *Rated R*, Rihanna wanted to have fun with her next album. A happier album, *Loud*, came out in 2010. Rihanna was on a roll. She released more albums in 2011 and 2012. *Talk That Talk* and *Unapologetic* topped the charts as well.

BATTLESHIP

Rihanna's main dream was music. But she was interested in acting, too. In 2012, she appeared in the movie *Battleship*. She played an officer. Her character had to help save the planet.

In 2011, Rihanna became the youngest artist to have 10 No. 1 hits. She was just 23 years old.

Rihanna's eighth album came out in 2016. When making it, she tried taking more risks. But she also wanted the songs to feel timeless. Her plan worked. *ANTI* hit No. 1 on Billboard's album chart. Rihanna worked with rapper Drake on the song "Work." The song earned two Grammy nominations. Rihanna said *ANTI* was her best album.

NICKNAMES

Rihanna's fandom is called the Navy. Rihanna chose the name herself. She said her fans include all sorts of people, just like the real navy. The fans have a nickname for Rihanna, too. They call her "RiRi." Her friends still call her Robyn.

Drake presents Rihanna with an award at the 2016 MTV Video Music Awards.

In the Spotlight
"UMBRELLA"

Rihanna's biggest hit was "Umbrella." But the song was offered to two other artists first. Both turned it down. Rihanna heard a demo of the song and loved it. She asked to sing it. Producers agreed. They began recording. Right away, they knew it was the right choice.

Listeners liked it, too. The song topped the Billboard Hot 100 chart for seven weeks. It was one of 2007's biggest songs. Over the years, the song gathered more and more views and streams. It stayed famous for many years.

> Rihanna has performed "Umbrella" many times. She even sang it during her Super Bowl halftime show.

In 2017, Rihanna was featured on Kendrick Lamar's song "Loyalty." The two artists won a Grammy for the song.

BRANCHING OUT

After 2016, Rihanna started many new projects. She still made music. But for a while, it was only as a guest artist. She appeared on other artists' songs. But Rihanna didn't release more albums.

In the late 2010s, Rihanna put more time into acting. She landed a role in the TV show *Bates Motel*. She played Marion Crane in two episodes. Rihanna appeared in a few movies, too. The biggest was *Ocean's 8*. It was an action comedy. It told the story of a gang of thieves.

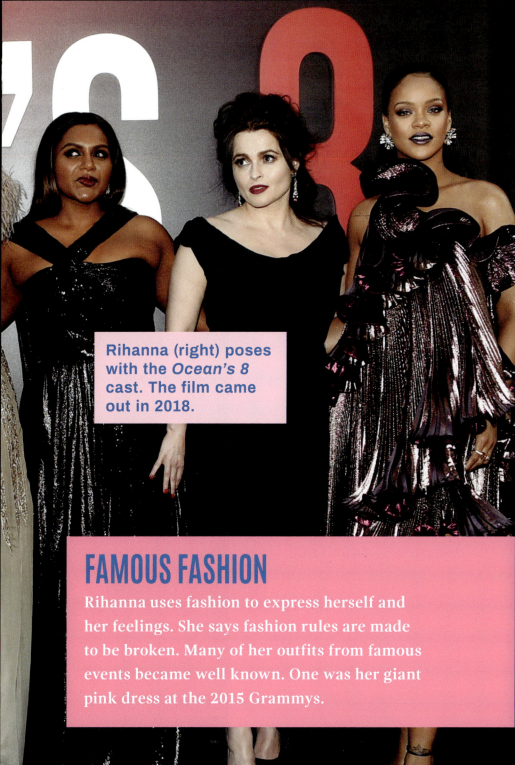

Rihanna (right) poses with the *Ocean's 8* cast. The film came out in 2018.

FAMOUS FASHION

Rihanna uses fashion to express herself and her feelings. She says fashion rules are made to be broken. Many of her outfits from famous events became well known. One was her giant pink dress at the 2015 Grammys.

In 2017, Rihanna started one of her biggest projects yet. She created her own makeup company. It was called Fenty Beauty. The brand offered 40 colors of makeup. The tones went from pale to dark. The company was an instant success. Products sold quickly. Many people found shades that matched their skin.

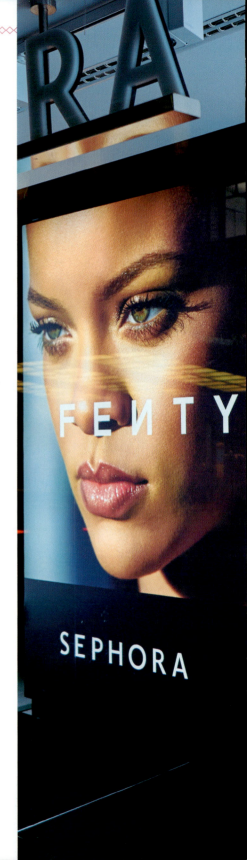

In 2018, Rihanna started a clothing line called Savage X Fenty. The clothes came in many sizes. They matched many different skin colors, too. Like Fenty Beauty, Savage X Fenty did very well. People thought the clothes were comfortable but still looked good. In 2021, Rihanna became a billionaire.

FAMILY TIME

Near the end of 2020, Rihanna began dating rapper A$AP Rocky. In 2022, the two started a family. They had a son. His name was RZA. Later, they had a second son, Riot.

Working with businesses such as Sephora helped Rihanna grow her wealth.

In 2023, Rihanna performed "Lift Me Up" at the Academy Awards.

48

In 2022, Rihanna finally released new music of her own. She co-wrote and sang "Lift Me Up." The song was for the movie *Black Panther: Wakanda Forever*. Then, in 2023, Rihanna returned to live performances in a big way. She performed at the 2023 Super Bowl halftime show. She set a Guinness World Record for viewers.

"LIFT ME UP"

"Lift Me Up" celebrated the life of Chadwick Boseman. The actor had played Black Panther in previous films. He passed away in 2020.

Chapter 6

A STRONG LEGACY

Through the early 2020s, Rihanna continued to be a global success. She won multiple awards around the world. And she had dozens of top 10 hits in the United States, the United Kingdom, and Australia.

In 2023, Rihanna became the first female artist to have 10 songs with a billion streams each on Spotify.

Rihanna co-wrote many of her biggest hits. She also helped write other songs throughout her career. Even when she doesn't write, Rihanna is very involved in her music. Being a central part of the creation is important to her.

A STAR WITH STYLE

Rihanna's fashion style has won awards. In 2014, she won an award for her own personal style. The presenter praised her bold and exciting choices. In 2019, her company won a major sportswear award. It honored Fenty for taking casual clothes to a new level.

Rihanna attends a fashion event in New York in 2023.

Over the years, Rihanna found many ways to give back. In 2012, she started the Clara Lionel Foundation. This group helps people who are harmed by climate change and natural disasters. Rihanna named it after her grandparents, Clara and Lionel.

HELPING OUT

Climate change often has a larger effect on people with less money. The Clara Lionel Foundation focuses on this situation in the Caribbean. It helps people get ready before natural disasters. The group helps fix buildings and improve emergency response systems.

In 2017, Rihanna won Harvard's Humanitarian of the Year Award for her work to help others.

By 2024, Rihanna had more than 150 million followers on Instagram.

By May 2023, Rihanna was worth $1.7 billion. Most of this money came from her companies. Rihanna tried to use that money for good. She continued donating to charities. She also kept working on new projects. Fans were excited to see what she would do next.

"NEVER A FAILURE"

Rihanna's life wasn't always easy. But she never gave up. She believes that is an important lesson. She even has a tattoo about it. It says, "Never a failure. Always a lesson."

FAST FACTS

Full name: Robyn Rihanna Fenty
Birth date: February 20, 1988
Birthplace: St. Michael, Barbados

TIMELINE

1988 — Robyn Rihanna Fenty is born on February 20.

2004 — Rihanna signs with Jay-Z and Def Jam Recordings.

2005 — Rihanna's first single, "Pon de Replay," is an international hit.

2007 — Rihanna receives her first Grammy Award.

2012 — Rihanna creates the Clara Lionel Foundation.

2017 — Rihanna creates Fenty Beauty.

2022 — Rihanna releases the song "Lift Me Up" for *Black Panther: Wakanda Forever*.

2023 — Rihanna performs at the Super Bowl halftime show.

COMPREHENSION QUESTIONS

Write your answers on a separate piece of paper.

1. Write a few sentences describing how Rihanna's music career began.

2. If you started a company, what would it make or sell? Why?

3. What was Rihanna's first single?
    - A. "Pon de Replay"
    - B. "Umbrella"
    - C. "Lift Me Up"

4. Why might climate change have a larger effect on people with less money?
    - A. It's easier for them to move to new places.
    - B. It's harder for them to pay for changes or repairs.
    - C. People with lots of money aren't affected by climate change.

5. What does **involved** mean in this book?

*Even when she doesn't write, Rihanna is very **involved** in her music. Being a central part of the creation is important to her.*

    A. paid very little money
    B. part of making something
    C. not part of making something

6. What does **tones** mean in this book?

*The brand offered 40 colors of makeup. The **tones** went from pale to dark.*

    A. shades of color
    B. types of sound
    C. very light colors

Answer key on page 64.

GLOSSARY

abusive
Cruel or violent toward others.

addict
A person who cannot stop using or doing something.

charities
Organizations set up to help people in need.

contract
An agreement to pay someone money, often for doing work.

demo
An early recording of a song.

genres
Types or categories of music.

immigrants
People who move to a new country.

platform
A raised surface.

producer
Someone who helps plan the making of music.

record label
A company that helps artists put out music.

represent
To be a symbol for a larger group of people.

single
A song released separately from an album. Singles are often promoted with music videos and radio play.

TO LEARN MORE

BOOKS

Abdo, Kenny. *Pop Music History*. Minneapolis: Abdo Publishing, 2020.

Huddleston, Emma. *Taylor Swift*. Mendota Heights, MN: Focus Readers, 2021.

Nnachi, Ngeri. *Changemakers in Music: Women Leading the Way*. Minneapolis: Lerner Publications, 2024.

ONLINE RESOURCES

Visit **www.apexeditions.com** to find links and resources related to this title.

ABOUT THE AUTHOR

Rebecca Kraft Rector is a former librarian and the author of more than 30 fiction and nonfiction books. She has written about space, forms of matter, reptiles, and many other subjects.

INDEX

ANTI, 36
A$AP Rocky, 46
Australia, 50
awards, 30, 50, 52

Barbados, 9–10, 17–18
Bates Motel, 42
Battleship, 34
Black Panther: Wakanda Forever, 49
Boseman, Chadwick, 49

Clara Lionel Foundation, 54

Def Jam Recordings, 20
Drake, 36

fashion, 43, 52
Fenty Beauty, 44, 46
Forde, Melissa, 15

Jay-Z, 20, 30

New York, 17–18
Ne-Yo, 30

Ocean's 8, 42

"Pon de Replay," 23, 26

reggae, 13, 26
Rogers, Evan, 17, 20, 23

Savage X Fenty, 46, 52
Stefani, Gwen, 24
Super Bowl, 5, 49

Timberlake, Justin, 30

"Umbrella," 30, 38
United Kingdom, 50
United States, 50

ANSWER KEY:
1. Answers will vary; 2. Answers will vary; 3. A; 4. B; 5. B; 6. A